Desktop Guide

to

Restoring Dignity

&

Leadership

Bart O. Davis

Desktop Guide to Restoring Dignity & Leadership

How to restore the dignity and leadership that have been engineered out of the workforce

A how-to manual for first-time supervisors and a refresher for leaders

Bart O. Davis

Copyright © 1999 by Bart O. Davis

All rights reserved.
This book may not be reproduced in whole or in part, by any means, including photocopying and electronic transmission, without written permission of the copyright holder.

Printed in the United States of America
Produced with assistance by Griffith Publishing
ISBN 0-9672130-0-2

For more information:
B&K Solutions
7049 Greenborough Dr.
PO Box 664
Midvale, Utah 84047
801 566-4596   1 888 668-LEAD (5323)
colbd@ix.netcom.com
www.leaderswin.com

Aknowledgments

I wish to acknowledge my family for their love and support during my sometimes inadequate attempts to live the principles in which I so strongly believe.

They have also been extremely supportive in my attempt to publish the principles that I hope will provide a better world for my grandchildren.

To my wife Kathy, daughters Dina and Danae and son Brandon and their families, THANK YOU.

Contents

Acknowledgments .... *v*
Preface .... *ix*
A Note from the Author .... *xiv*

PART I: WHAT WENT WRONG? 1
The McNamara Syndrome 3
Humanism or Abdication 8
Loss of Loyalty 11

PART II: WHAT WORKS 17
Dignity 18
Selflessness 22
Integrity 24
Responsibility 28
Pride 33
Training 35
What Nobody Really Teaches: Hiring
 and Firing 40
Urgency 43
Communication 46

**PART III: SIMPLE AND SUCCESSFUL
 LEADERSHIP** 50
Who: You and the Others 52
What 58
When 63
Where 70
Why 72

CONCLUSION 75

APPENDICES
Appendix I: Trust Cycle 77
Appendix II: Training Cycle 79
Appendix III: Leader's Checklist 80
Appendix IV: Recommended Reading 81
Appendix V: Expectations Sample 82
Appendix VI: Feedback Sample 84

Selected Bibliography 86

Preface

Many people have already said it in many ways, but I want to make it as clear as I possibly can: In my view, and for the purposes of this book, management and leadership are totally different disciplines. Good managers are not necessarily good leaders. Managers manage things, resources. Leaders lead people. If you consider people to be simply another resource, you will never attain your goals through management practices or meet the demands of your organization.

After the elation of a new promotion and following all of the congratulatory calls, what then? The realization hits you that all of your professional successes have been due to your personal effort and work ethic. You have worked and studied all of your life to achieve a position of leadership. However, it now occurs to you that you are ill prepared to assume responsibility for the success of others. How many times have you seen successful employees promoted into supervisory positions and then struggle and fail or quit in frustration? It doesn't have to happen. This guide will give you the basic traits you need to add to your arsenal of already obvious attributes.

I have wondered for years why leadership is not a required discipline taught as a core competency. If elementary leadership training had followed reading, writing, and arithmetic, and every graduate of elementary, secondary, and post-secondary education schools had a basic understanding of leadership skills, imagine what our country could be today. Somehow we allowed "elites" to lead us into the twentieth century and institutionalized the idea that the "rank and file" were not capable of leadership and taking individual responsibility. An unfortunate consequence of that institutionalization was the reduction of individual dignity and the demeaning of working men and women to be seen as just another commodity or resource to be used by the captains of industry.

Hard-working, intelligent, and dedicated employees who finally attain recognition and are promoted to managerial or supervisory positions because of their education, experience, abilities, and contributions in a particular field, often flounder and fail. They struggle because they do not understand the human dynamics and responsibilities incurred when becoming accountable for other people and their work. MBAs and PhDs, as well as anyone in a leadership position, find themselves wondering why they are spending so much time dealing with personnel problems. They believe instead that they should be putting their skills and knowledge to use in pursuit of organizational goals!

The problem is that we still haven't totally recognized the value of the individual worker. We haven't provided training and support for new supervisors. We simply promote them and watch as they try to compete with others in the same situation. Meanwhile, we bolster the human resource departments, increase the litigation budget, and wonder why the millions of dollars spent on the "feel good" programs we have been sending everyone to are not improving the workplace environment.

This guide is meant to be an aid to those who find themselves in a position of leadership for the first time. Perhaps it will also be of value to those already struggling with the responsibility of ensuring success to themselves, their co-workers, and the organization for which they work.

Two things a new leader needs to understand: First, unless you can and will take personal responsibility for your own successes and failures, and the failures of your subordinates, you will never be a leader. Second, you must be a leader with or without the support of your superiors. Most quality, modernization, and change programs fail in business because they are not truly supported by the leadership of the organization. If your supervisor did not give you this book, you may be facing an uphill battle.

Why are self-help books, seminars, and the consulting profession such a significant part of our culture? Why do people spend millions of dollars and thousands of hours looking for the secrets to being successful team leaders, supervisors, and managers? It is apparent to me that regardless of our education and experience, we feel inadequate. We believe or hope there is an expert that can give us the solution to our problems. Unfortunately, **it is impossible for others to fulfill our leadership obligations.**

It occurred to me as I looked at the shelves of books around my office, most of which are highly rated management and self-improvement publications, that something has yet to be explained. The conclusion I reached is both simple and personal:

We do not want to believe that leadership is what is missing.

I have read and studied the works of dozens of recognized management authorities. If you take away the intellectual and literary efforts they have used to differentiate themselves, the core messages are basically the same. Some are presented more eloquently or entertainingly than others, but nevertheless they are similar.

This book is not for the coffee table and is not intended to be an issue for academic debate and review. It is a simple guide to help mere mortals. It is for men and women who find themselves dealing with the day-to-day realities of being responsible for other people's successes and well being. Their future is dependent on how well they meet their new responsibilities and the resulting interpersonal relationships. It is for people who are excellent employees who suddenly find themselves in leadership positions with little or no leadership training.

You will undoubtedly notice throughout this book different examples that have military connotations. They are the results of experiences I have had throughout the world during my 34-year military career. In most instances, they bring a point right to center stage. However, this is not a book on military leadership. The military has suffered from the same maladies of over-management and lack of human understanding as has the civilian sector. It has experienced the same assaults on human dignity as has the rest of society. Our entire society is struggling to maintain the greatness of America and its leadership. Industry, technology, and the government are all trying to regain the human spirit that has been "engineered out" of the workplace over the past sixty to eighty years.

Preface

It takes leadership to get into a competitive position. Leaders understand there is no such thing as "human resources," but rather human beings with individual hopes, fears, personal integrity, and desires to be productive, valuable participants in society. Millions of dollars have been spent trying to empower the workforce rather than reinforcing and implementing the simplest, most basic and time-tested interpersonal theory–*the golden rule*. (Simply stated, treat people like you would like to be treated.)

This book is based on the following premise that I have personally proven and seen demonstrated time after time at all levels of government, business and other enterprises:

> "People will always exceed expectations, good or bad."

If people are treated with dignity and believe they will receive credit and be rewarded for their good work, they will work hard and will always exceed what is expected of them.

However, if people are treated in a demeaning manner, do not clearly understand your expectations, or are not recognized for their good work, they will exceed your low expectations on the negative side of the scale.

There are very few bad workers—just untrained leaders.

A Note from the Author

Regarding gender: I have struggled for hours attempting to make this guide as lucid and meaningful as possible. Only after numerous attempts to incorporate both masculine and feminine genders have I decided to stop worrying about being politically correct and write it from my point of view. I am hopeful that anyone (man or woman) seriously reading a book on leadership will not take personal offense. Any use of a masculine pronoun applies equally to both genders. I assure you it has been my experience that gender has nothing to do with the leadership abilities a person possesses. People of both genders excel and fail miserably.

Throughout this guide, you will find phrases and thoughts printed in **bold**. These were printed intentionally in this manner to highlight important points that need to be reviewed and reinforced often.

PART I

What Went Wrong?

A short review of the history of American industrial growth, management approaches, and results is appropriate to understand where we are today. To paraphrase Lewis Carroll, without knowing where you are and how you got there, it is extremely difficult to know what to do to get where you need to be.

The maladies of today's workforce and America's ability to compete internationally are a direct result of the conscious "engineering out" of self-reliance, initiative, individual dignity, and honesty. They also stem from an "elitist" approach to management born at the onset of the Industrial Revolution.

We continue to rationalize that individual workers are not capable of taking responsibility for themselves. We continue to use "elitist" approaches to motivation, such as the myth of empowerment, to let employees think they have some significant impact when they do not. We try to give the impression that there is some connection or bond between us and the customer beyond the self-interests that are served. In addition, we continue to talk about employer loyalty as if dedication or ability will preserve the workforce's long-term employment. We hedge on being totally honest and accepting the truth about what is needed. The hard reality is that **each employee must take individual responsibility** for his own future. **Your future is only secure as long as you are providing value** to the consumers of your efforts, the products or services you produce, and the people around you.

Chapter 1

The McNamara Syndrome

The men and women who immigrated to this country and settled it brought America into greatness. These people were self sufficient and able to evaluate changing situations. They acted without thinking beyond what was the right thing to do at the time for themselves, their families, and their employers. The vast majority of those decisions were not selfish but were made after considering the personal and societal benefits of their actions. Each individual was personally responsible for himself, his family, occupation, and community.

"Yankee ingenuity," as it has been called, contributed in no small part to this country becoming a world leader in the few short years between its founding and the late 1800s.

Freedom, the pursuit of happiness, and the original ideal of all men being created equal were the very reasons for mass immigration to the United States. These ideals and principles led to the unleashing of human talent and ambition. Release from the caste system domination that had controlled daily living in the countries from which the immigrants came allowed the remarkable expansion in personal and national growth and wealth.

Unfortunately, there are always those who believe that a certain class of society is somehow more able and worthy than all others. Human nature being what it is, these people go about initiating the process of gaining control. Thus it has been throughout history and thus it still is in America today.

Let me hasten to say that most of the early pioneers of management control processes did not necessarily initiate control for evil purposes. Rather, the concept evolved as a consequence of mass production and necessity. A flaw occurred, however, when the human element simply became just another resource available to management. Dignity and personal responsibility were not part of modern management considerations taught by business schools and universities in the early 1900s. In fact, management systems were designed to control resources, assure profits, and decentralize operating responsibility while centralizing planning and controls. Early systems of management control and scientific management were developed to operate mass manufacturing at a time when legions of immigrants flooded the workforce. Managers were taught to treat workers like human machines who could perform only simple and limited tasks.

Robert S. McNamara, former president of Ford Motor Company and U.S. Secretary of Defense, is one of the highest profile examples of the results of scientific management processes. He believed that the most effective organizations were those in which subordinates simply obeyed, and that only men at the top had the right information to make decisions.

The effect was to disempower foremen, engineers, craftsmen, and workers on assembly lines. When he left the company that brought America the Edsel, he took with him that same attitude and education to run the Department of Defense. There he employed his "superior" education and intellect to manage and control the first defeat the U.S. military had ever suffered.

McNamara made an extraordinary remark about "managing reality" as late as his February 1967 speech at Millsaps College. He extolled management as "the most creative of all the arts, for its medium is human talent itself," and referred to it as the "gate" for spreading change through society. He further stated, "The real threat to democracy comes from under-management, not from over-management. To under-manage reality is not to keep it free. It is simply to let some force other than reason shape reality."

McNamara's theory of over-management is an example of the **belief by elitists that it is their divine right and obligation to ensure Americans are not under-managed.**

Peter F. Drucker in his book, *The Practice of Management,* makes this statement:

> ". . . management is not only grounded in the nature of the modern industrial system and in the needs of the modern business enterprise to which an industrial system must entrust its productive resources–both human and material. It [management] also expresses basic beliefs of modern Western society. It expresses the belief in the possibility of controlling man's livelihood through systematic organization of economic resources. It [management] expresses the belief that economic change can be made in the most

powerful engine for human betterment and social justice... Management, which is the organ of society specifically charged with making resources productive; that is, with the responsibility for organized economic advance, thereafter reflects the basic spirit of the modern age."

It is evident that those early management pioneers' view of and trust in **statistical control and management theory have not been the ultimate answer** to all of our social and economic challenges.

Leadership is not quantifiable; therefore, it is somewhat outside the intellectual realm of academia. Positive leadership is possibly the highest achievement that can be obtained through the pure strength of character, intellect, and an understanding of human nature. Throughout history, it has been leaders—not managers—who have changed entire civilizations. Now at the beginning of the twenty-first century, we have come to the realization that the highly acclaimed management controls of the early and mid 1900s alone cannot achieve the goal of reflecting the basic spirit of the modern age.

A quick study of the life of Robert S. McNamara will illustrate how intellectual arrogance led to the "engineering out" of human dignity and an increasing desire for power. Under the noble banner of societal protection or improvement, and astride the charging stallion of capitalism and profitability, one can quickly succumb to the intoxicating and addicting need for control and ever-increasing power. Ultimately tighter and tighter control leads to covert (even subconscious) revolution, decreasing effort, and an ever-increasing loss of loyalty or feeling of obligation.

Even the omniscient McNamara with his legions of MBAs, PhDs, and generals could not manage to preclude the natural outcome of human engineering. His systems of control failed just as other methods throughout history have failed when attempting to suppress the human spirit. There never has been, or ever can be, a truly lasting and great society or organization when the human spirit and individual dignity are restrained.

When someone believes he knows what is better for another, and through some position of power forces that other person to act against his natural instincts, a degradation of the human spirit will ultimately manifest itself in unacceptable workplace behavior. The same is true in any segment of society inside and outside of the workplace.

The human spirit was officially relegated, albeit not necessarily with malicious intent, to just another management principle by Frederick W. Taylor in *Shop Management* (1919).

> "Each man must learn to give up his particular way of doing things. . . adopt his methods to the many new standards and grow accustomed to receiving and obeying instructions covering details, large and small, which in the past have been left to individual judgment."

Through our modern-day remedies, we're looking for ways to re-energize the human spirit. We are trying hard to overcome the philosophy that each person must give up his individuality. This general philosophy has been an essential part of the American industrial processes and is even now part of the technological management processes.

Chapter 2

Humanism or Abdication

America's manufacturing capabilities in the mid and late 1940s created opportunities for the captains of industry that propelled us into world domination. Scientific management methods of the earlier decades were touted as successful, as proved by unprecedented profits and growth. The void left by the devastation of war in other parts of the world and the American ability to produce consumer goods painted a picture of success that many attributed to Statistical Quality Control.

As the decades passed and the countries of Europe, Asia, and other areas of the world rebuilt and improved their industrial base, business owners began to challenge the arrogance and belief that America was ordained to be the universal supplier of goods. Growing international competition caused a reevaluation of the management processes that had been undisputed by the highly educated and corporately trained captains of industry.

Humanism or Abdication

Most dedicated men and women who spend their youth in the pursuit of knowledge and rise to positions of educators, executives, and other professionals in American society serve us well. We enjoy an unprecedented standard of living as a result of their belief that they are part of something great and are providing service. Individually and nationally we profit from their efforts in every phase of our lives. However, **the missing component** in their disciplines that we are desperately trying to discover **is the human element of dignity in the workforce.**

Cases can be made for other problems that have existed, but during my adult lifetime, the one overriding challenge has been how to reinstate dignity and individual responsibility into the workforce. The void has been recognized by many notable men and women throughout the years, but perhaps one of the first to sound the alarm was Dr. W. Edwards Deming.

He realized in the late 1940s that statistical methods alone could not produce quality products. Although known as a distinguished statistician, Deming was ignored by American industry until he appeared in a television documentary in 1980. The Deming message finally got out:

> "If you get gains in productivity only because people work smarter, not harder, that is total profit, and it multiplies several times."

The term "people working smarter" ignited a search for meaning that rages even today. Six plus decades of deprogramming "Yankee ingenuity" has left the working population with a void in understanding the work ethic required for success. Just as damning is our inability to capture and reestablish that ethic.

Multimillion-dollar enterprises have emerged. Publishers, philosophers, educators, consultants, and even theologians have blanketed the country espousing programs and methods for getting people to work smarter. A few examples are Quality Circles, Management by Objective, Total Quality Management, Participative Management, ISO 9000, reinventing, re-engineering, and on and on. What is wrong? What is missing? Why can't we recognize that what is called for is not another system or elitist-induced program, but rather the simple human traits of honesty, dignity, personal value, and self control?

Many improvements have occurred in the workplace in recent years as a result of quality improvement programs. However, individual employee benefits are more a result of efforts to gain short-term stability and profits than provide real culturally changing attitudes.

We are still abdicating our responsibilities as leaders and managers. We want to hire the solution rather than correct it ourselves. We want to have the workers change their habits, take responsibility, improve the quality of our products and services, and at the same time be loyal and happy. However, we don't completely yet believe we need to relinquish the power and perks we have worked so hard to obtain. In fact, we have developed a culture of seminar attenders. We judge ourselves by the amount of dollars spent and hours scheduled for self-improvement programs. We take great pride in announcing that we believe in empowering our workforce—and yet, what has really changed in the past decade?

Are we truly trying to be a more humanistic society or are we abdicating our responsibilities as leaders to the current roster of change consultants?

Chapter 3

Loss of Loyalty

In my view, the most overused and deceptive term of recent years is empowerment. Empowerment is defined as "investing with power, especially legal power, or official authority." When people are told that they are empowered, they automatically have an expectation that their leaders will confide in them and that their input will be valued and considered. They are led to believe that somehow, regardless of their experience and education, they will have some significant say in the administration and operations of the workplace. They are led to believe that initiative will be supported and rewarded.

The fatal flaw to empowerment is that the parameters are rarely, if ever, defined specifically to the particular workplace. With one exception, I have never heard of training that instructs managers on how to relinquish power to subordinates. Therefore, after the hype, which usually equates to the introduction of "The New Program," whichever one happens to be in vogue, expectations are raised to an unattainable and unrealistic level. From the outset, the best that can be hoped for is minimal harm to morale and to the quality and quantity of output from a disillusioned workforce because heightened expectations once again are not met.

The concept of empowerment results in the reduction of the authority of supervisors but not in their responsibility. It reduces personal responsibility and distributes it throughout the workplace to anonymous "they" or "them" entities who seldom have had appropriate training to meet the challenges of today's workplace.

People, regardless of their station in life, all want and need leadership, role models, mentors, or just someone to believe in. Instead of spending time trying to give power to employees who really don't want it, why not just step up and be a leader? Everyone will be happier.

If you are wondering whether to read any further, just read the next two or three sentences. After two decades of a fairly intensive bombardment of total quality, team involvement, participative management, and learning organization training by so-called experts, employment litigation has exploded. The number of lawsuits has risen by more than 2,200 percent and now accounts for an estimated one-fifth of all civil suits filed in U.S. courts. This epidemic of employment litigation is sure to worsen as the workforce continues to grow more diverse. I am convinced that instead of another committee to study the problem and make recommendations, what we need is a serious review and illustration of what makes people successful.

Everyone who has studied the workforce in America understands that even the most sincere pledge of future employment, the hallmark of IBM for so many years, is unrealistic in today's environment. Everyone from the CEO to the newest dock worker in any organization understands that there are forces beyond their control that could cause their jobs to disappear by next month. Why then, do we pretend that everything is all right? Why do we go through our daily lives without acknowledging that we may need to change jobs? The fact is, there is far less job security today than in the past. We shouldn't allow workers to continue to believe in the fairy tale of lifelong employment in one position or with the same organization. If they are dealt with honestly, workers are capable of displaying the dedication and loyalty that they need for business to compete. They can also understand the necessity of increasing their own value.

We need the **simple truth: that we, individually, are dependent on the success of each other** for our futures—every line worker, clerical worker, tradesman, salesman, or executive. With the realization of a critical interdependency, we can begin to learn how we need to relate to each other. We can also learn how to best fulfill our own personal responsibilities toward our fellow workers—not as superiors or subordinates, but as fellow workers. By fulfilling these responsibilities, we can understand, reinforce, and improve our own value and ensure that our talents and services are going to be required in the future.

There is a false notion that you have customers everywhere—internal customers, external customers, even customer's customers. Over the past few years, I have spent as much time filling out customer satisfaction surveys as I have tax forms—and to what end?

The rock bottom truth is that **you (as an individual) are your only customer.** Everyone else is simply a consumer. Your employer consumes your time, talent, and effort. The purchaser of the service or product you produce consumes only to the extent that you are fulfilling his personal needs. There is no loyalty beyond the personal value that you individually give to those who pay you for your work, and those who pay you for and consume the products of your efforts. Therefore, you need to **empower yourself**. Don't wait another day for someone's permission to **take personal responsibility for your future**.

It is not selfish to recognize that you are your only customer. To add value to yourself is not the same as taking an "everyone-for-himself" attitude at the expense of others. **The only real way you can truly take care of yourself is to assure everyone around you is successful**. By so doing, you add value to everyone.

The employee loyalty and security of the past, as provided by IBM, GM, and even the government, are not part of the realities of the next millennium. I'm not casting blame on anyone but only trying to point out that we need to stop trying to find a painless way to explain to people that their futures can best be assured by taking individual responsibility for themselves. People must demonstrate personal value to those who wish to consume their efforts or benefit from the product or service they provide.

Personal value can best be gained through working in harmony with your human instincts and by learning from leaders who understand the value and needs of people. We can no longer afford to believe that someone else will take care of us. Simply showing up at work and doing what you are told is a dangerous way to plan your future. Management concepts are valuable and necessary, but it is time to place leaders—not just managers—into every position responsible for other people's motivation. We do a great job of turning out MBAs, lawyers, doctors, and scientists of every kind. We still lead the world in most professional categories. Our standard of living is the envy of the world. Nevertheless, we do not train our workforce how to lead or, just as critical, how to follow. We are so intent on building consensus that we have lost sight of basic leadership and individual responsibility. Our society and organizations are being run by committees. Somebody has to be in charge!

I know of no organization where petty politics, workplace conflict, rumor mongering, and other such activities do not dominate the workforce. Real leadership, leading to a true appreciation for oneself and the value of fellow workers, would resolve the vast majority of these problems over time and increase the production capability of any organization almost immediately.

Leadership qualities are not necessarily inherited. Some people are fortunate to have certain natural aptitudes and tendencies that enable them to easily recognize and implement activities that are appreciated by others. However, for those not fortunate enough to have those natural abilities, a few basic truths will suffice to ensure a successful beginning, especially for those who find themselves in leadership positions for the first time.

Regardless of how you have been treated or what you think of the leadership styles of those for whom you have worked, remember this: **In today's workforce, you must lead, not command or manage!**

Everyone understands that their new boss does not have all the answers. This is particularly true if the new boss is a first-time supervisor, team leader, or manager. Most people are willing to be supportive at first. They wait and watch to see what kind of person has just been entrusted with their future. The challenge for new supervisors/managers is to gain the trust, respect, and loyalty of those over whom they have been placed. I have found that you can get desired results through command, intimidation, and various other positional or authoritarian methods. However, doing so compromises your long-term possibilities in exchange for short-term gain. Short-term gains at the expense of loyalty and support will erode your future abilities for success and devalue your personal worth in the eyes of those who work for you. Subordinate loyalty and support are the most valuable elements you can have as a supervisor. If you believe you are intelligent or powerful enough to gain their best efforts through sheer force of your will, remember this: Regardless of what you achieve, it will be less than what it could have been if fully supported by your charges.

Loyalty is earned, not directed. One of the truths of leadership is that people will willingly follow and be loyal to a leader they believe is trustworthy. It is up to the new supervisor/manager to earn that trust. (See Appendix I—Trust Cycle)

The next nine chapters are not concepts for leadership experimentation, but are rather leadership traits and principles that have been proven over and over again. Individuals perceive and implement them through their own filters and abilities. As a basis for new supervisors, these concepts will not lead you astray. For the older and more experienced managers and executives, they may be worth reviewing if you are not enjoying pure workplace harmony, productivity, and unqualified employee loyalty.

PART II

What Works

The following attributes are not intended to be all-inclusive or serve as the definitive work on leadership. You can spend a lifetime on the study of leadership and what has made various leaders successful. I have attempted to give you in this guide, and particularly in this and the following section, what I consider the basic elements of leadership. I have tried to illustrate how they have affected my life and the lives of others I have known. In addition, I have selected these attributes because they have been valuable aids in securing a comfortable and peaceful life. Perhaps they have also contributed, in a small but positive way, to the organizations we have been fortunate enough to have been associated with.

Chapter 4

Dignity

Dignity is the quality of being worthy of esteem or respect. It is the absolute **bedrock of leadership.** Dignity is a necessary and vital component of every successful relationship. It is vital to both the leader and to those being led. Without dignity and mutual respect, both parties labor under an illusion. The worker pretends to care about the success of the organization, and the supervisor pretends to care for the welfare of the worker. Neither is able to reach a satisfying level in the relationship because they both know, if only subconsciously, that the relationship is based on an illusion. There is no boundary or level low enough that precludes the need for dignity. There is no amount of fame, notoriety, responsibility, or authority that can be achieved where dignity is not critical.

What does this mean to the new supervisor who simply wants to know how to get started on the right foot? **You need to realize that your success depends on the success of your subordinates.** You cannot be any more successful than the least successful of those for whom you are responsible.

Although it may appear phony and self-serving at first to show concern and interest and inquire into the feelings of subordinates, something reciprocal takes place. When people are acknowledged and recognized as a valuable member of your organization, they start to act the part. The reciprocal benefits are that they will genuinely become concerned about you, your welfare, and your success.

It should come as no surprise that when people sincerely care about one another, little things are done without having to be asked or without any thought of reward. It is human nature.

By acknowledging subordinates, learning to truly care about their feelings, and expressing confidence in their abilities, you demonstrate respect for their value to you and to your organization. That demonstration fosters the employee's self-respect and loyalty, which increases his value both to himself and to you.

Great leaders sometimes are demanding, harsh, and can perhaps even be characterized as brutal, but they are great and successful because those for whom they have responsibility know that they care. They take necessary actions only after considering the consequences to their followers. They do not make the hard decisions for personal gain, but for the well being of the organization and for its members.

General George S. Patton was a great leader, say what you will. I have not met a man who was under his command who is not proud of the fact. Those men know that **leadership does not necessarily mean being liked**, but **it does mean being respected and trusted**. That same dignity and pride that is now over fifty years old is as powerful today as it was when it was used to win and end World War II.

Dignity and pride are much the same: you must be proud of being a leader. Being a leader places a special trust in you. You need to take pride in your people, in the results of their efforts, and in your operation. Those for whom you now have responsibility also need to be proud of you. The genuine respect you have for each other is the intangible element that produces products and services which cannot possibly be matched by anyone who does not have dignity in the workplace.

I am not a Marine, but I have been in awe all of my life at the universal pride and dignity of Marines. I certainly am not implying that the new supervisor or manager should try to mirror the Marine Corps' methods of leadership, but it is noteworthy. New privates and field grade officers all exude the same feelings of caring, trusting, common purpose, and loyalty. I am sure it is a result of instilling dignity in each individual and having a real concern for their well being and success.

I recently observed the ritual of a highly respected and nationally recognized leader in action. I have seen this ritual many times, and always by people I admired. The gentleman entered a room filled with men and women, most of whom he had never met before. The purpose of the meeting was to get the audience to approve a new board, with him as the president. Rather than entering with fanfare and proceeding to the seat that had been prepared for him at the head table, he stopped and started introducing himself to the attendees who were seated at the back of the hall, much to the consternation of his escorts. He then proceeded to walk around the tables and personally introduced himself to everyone in the room and shook their hands.

He did not portray himself as a man of power or wealth or as a person of national prominence, but simply as a man who recognized the value of every person in the hall. That simple acknowledgment and handshake displayed his understanding of the need for dignity. He, with that simple courtesy, won enough trust and respect to easily be placed in a position of leadership by those in attendance.

Chapter 5

Selflessness

Selflessness is the unselfish act of doing something for someone that nobody expects or knows about. A hallmark of a true leader is someone who goes about taking care of and watching out for the well being of those for whom they are responsible, without regard to credit.

A few years ago my wife had the privilege of working for a truly great leader. In the few short social and professional encounters I had with him, I learned valuable lessons that provided benchmarks and many qualities to emulate. Selflessness was just one. During that time, my wife's mother passed away from cancer. The normal courtesies were extended. Flowers, cards, and obligatory phone calls were received with routine expressions of sympathy.

My wife was politely informed that her loss was her immediate priority and to not be concerned about returning to work until she felt up to it. The funeral was out of state and several hours travel from our home under normal conditions, but the day of the funeral was *not* normal. A midwinter snowstorm practically stopped traffic in two states.

Selflessness

As friends and family gathered in preparation for the service, I noticed a familiar face in the back of the chapel. The man for whom my wife worked, the director of a large state division, had taken the time and made the effort to travel through the storm. No one would have known had I not noticed him standing in the back, simply showing his personal concern and respect for our family.

What do you think is our opinion of this man? Could any leader ever do anything that could possibly cause us to be more loyal or supportive than this simple, yet extraordinarily selfless act?

As a new supervisor, you will soon be known for your personal traits. No amount of training or education will be able to conceal your true character. You will become known as a person who works in everyone's best interest and who should be supported or else you will earn a reputation as a taker and a user who must be tolerated.

Always remember, it is better to stand in the back of the chapel and make sure everyone is taken care of than to stand in the front and preside over mediocrity.

Chapter 6

Integrity

It has been said that integrity and honesty are simply doing the right thing when no one is watching. Let me give you a short anecdote as to how I came to a way of life that has served me well.

My father at one time in his life drove a bakery truck. Dad partially loaded the truck with rolls and bread at a bakery in our hometown, then drove it to another city where pies were made. He finished loading the truck with pies and then transported the whole load to a large distribution point in yet another city, for general delivery by local delivery vans.

When I was six or seven, I was allowed to ride with Dad while he was completing his nightly ritual. I believed I was a great help and looked forward to riding in the big truck and feeling like a grown-up. In retrospect, I slept most of the time and required supervision. Dad had to make sure I didn't get hurt around the machinery used to load and unload the large racks filled with baked goods. I always felt my help was critical to the success of the night's assignments. It was a special treat to

Integrity

spend time with my Dad, who it seemed was always either working or sleeping. It was just me and Dad making a living for the family.

It was about a four-hour drive from the pie shop to the distribution point. One night while on my support duties, I awoke to find the truck parked in front of the distribution warehouse. Dad had already started to unload it. As I got out and looked around, I saw that he was in the back of the warehouse unloading some racks. It was about two or three in the morning and it had been some time since I had last eaten. Right in front of me by the door to the warehouse was a large rack filled with pies—hundreds of cherry and berry pies. It appeared to me to be most logical and innocent to simply help myself to one of those pies. Those pies were good, and who would ever know or miss one of hundreds of those little pies? So I helped myself. When Dad returned to the truck for another rack, the pie was almost gone. There I was, right in the middle of an industrial area at three in the morning, just me, my Dad, and a rack of hundreds of pies—minus one.

The events of the next few minutes impacted my life as much as anything I can remember. Dad walked over, surveyed the situation, and asked me who had given me the pie. I responded that no one had given it to me; I had just helped myself. I further mentioned that nobody could possibly ever miss just one pie out of those hundreds. No one could or would ever know. Dad kneeled down, straightened up my coat, took the paper wrapping I was holding, looked me in the eye and said, "*You* know. You took something that was not yours; the size or the amount doesn't matter. Who knows or doesn't is not important. You are either honest or dishonest. Either you can be trusted or you can't.

Never confuse right and wrong with who knows what you are doing, or with the value of an item. You know right and wrong, and you will be known throughout your life for how you keep your word and by the trust you will be given."

Dad took a dime out of his pocket (the price of the pie) and gave it to me. "Go put this on the table next to the office door," he said. "Remember that you almost ruined your life, lost your integrity, and could never be truly trusted by anyone, all for the price of a pie."

To this day, as I have throughout my life when faced with an opportunity to do something that could be considered as less than honest, or whenever there is a simple question of right or wrong, I ask myself: First, "who will know?" Second, "is my integrity worth any amount of money, let alone the price of a pie?"

If two weeks before Christmas you find an envelope of cash on the sidewalk and wonder if you should try and find the owner; or if the young clerk at the supermarket gives you too much in change; or if your office has a cabinet full of computer parts that you desperately need at home; you don't have to make a decision about what is the right thing to do. Who will know if you don't do the right thing? You will!

As a new supervisor, you should fully understand that by accepting your position, you automatically place yourself in a leadership role. By definition, leaders are examples. It is inevitable that the integrity and character displayed by the leader will be reflected by the organization that they oversee. The character of the leader will not only be reflected by the organization, but it also tends to be magnified (good or bad). You should weigh every act as to how it will be viewed by your employees. They believe whatever you do is all right for them to do. People will follow. Make sure that you are leading them in the right direction! Don't ever get in a position of making a decision just because it is legal. Recent history vividly illustrates the difference between legal and right. Always ask yourself, "Is it the right thing to do?" Also, "If your actions appeared in the newspaper, would you be comfortable defending them?"

Chapter 7

Responsibility

Responsibility means taking credit for your actions, good or bad. No excuses, no blame, just forthright honest **acceptance of the consequences of your actions**. What a simple, straightforward approach to your daily living this implies. What a timesaving concept this suggests. If people could use the time being spent trying to affix blame, production would be increased considerably. Nationally, it could equate to another workforce.

The single, most significant, personal trait contributing to the current state of our society is the reluctance or inability of individuals to seek and take personal responsibility for their actions. That inability or reluctance is cancerous. The decline in people believing they have personal responsibility, I believe, can be traced in large part to the engineering-out of responsibility in the early twentieth century workplaces. Also, the government contributed when it decided we weren't capable of taking care of ourselves and started to degrade our self-reliance through the implementation of government-managed retirement, welfare, and managed-care programs.

Abdication of personal responsibility grew to more of a societal norm in the 1960s and 70s, thanks to the "if it feels good, do it" mentality of that era. It led to giving little or no thought to the consequences of individual actions. The followers of popular pediatricians of the time raised the current generation of floundering leaders. These leaders are having trouble accepting responsibility for the quality of their personal work output, family relations, and even personal conduct. They are still reluctant to assign and require personal accountability. Establishing process action teams and diffusing responsibility can no longer substitute for a leader who can and will make decisions when an enterprise is losing market share and laying off significant numbers of its workforce.

Open any newspaper and pick the name of any successful corporate CEO, any private business person who is doing well, even a truly good government leader, and you will find a person who not only accepts responsibility but also pursues it.

Ask any personnel director how difficult it is to find someone who understands, let alone seeks, responsibility. Ask any manager or supervisor what a pleasure it is to have an employee who accepts responsibility, seeks additional challenges, and reaches beyond those elements in their position descriptions. Most people today simply want a job. They don't want to think or plan. They don't want to step outside of their comfort zone to assist or promote improvements. Their lives are outside of the workplace. Pursuing and accepting responsibility will place you in a small group with whom you have to compete.

Current remuneration systems, in most cases, discourage real initiative; only a few truly reward it. Appraisal and reward systems are a study and problem all their own. For our purpose here, you simply have to accept the responsibility of doing the best possible job you can, given the system in use by your employer.

If a person is not able or willing to stand up and **accept personal responsibility,** he does not have the basis to be considered for leadership positions. He should not even attempt to attain a supervisory position. It is not fair to him and certainly not to any unfortunate soul who may have to work under his direction. People who can't accept personal responsibility spend their time looking for something or someone to blame for their daily struggles. Leaders are not only responsible for themselves, but they are also responsible for those over whom they have authority. The best leaders spend their time finding ways to improve things, not trying to find something or someone to blame when things go wrong.

As mentioned earlier, much has been said and written about empowerment. Empowerment is nothing more than a contemporary term to mask the reality of a society that has grown up without the concept of individual responsibility being part of their formative training. It's a modern word that means it is permissible to be responsible for yourself. You now have permission to think for yourself. Well, you don't need permission. **Stand up and take control of your own future!**

You will be a successful leader if you have the dignity to stand and accept the consequences of your actions. You will be respected for your courage and admired by those who go through life blaming their poor lot on fate or some other myth. Be one of those special people who understands **you cannot always be right** and that **you will make mistakes** in the pursuit of progress. Be willing to give it your best and let the results stand. These are some of the most value-added attributes you can possess.

This short illustration will show the value of taking personal responsibility. Many years ago when I was working for General Motors Acceptance Corporation, I worked with two credit supervisors. Both had similar education, experience, and family background. Both had been successful and both had been transferred two or three times to different offices and positions. One always believed he had received the best job in the corporation, his new house was a castle, the neighbors were truly outstanding, and the schools were much better than the last place he had lived. We will call him Bob.

Bob took the responsibility of moving, establishing himself with fellow workers and neighbors, and making his home what he wanted it to be. The other, who we will call Carl, didn't like his new jobs. It seemed like the Corporation was out to get him. His new house wasn't as nice as his last one, the neighbors weren't as friendly, and his kids didn't get along in the new school. It wasn't Carl's fault that things never worked out; it was always someone else's fault.

Bob not only accepted responsibility for his lot in life, but also pursued more and more of it. Carl was always blaming someone for his problems.

I watched in amazement over the years how success seemed to follow Bob. Everyone around him was attracted to him; he was constantly receiving employment offers and invitations to join various organizations. Carl's career, on the other hand, seemed to stall. His negative approach to work and life in general resulted in people not wanting to be around him. Bob ended up as a top executive for one of the major automobile manufacturers in the world. Carl, the last time I heard, was working in a parts department in a small town. I'm sure he's still trying to figure out whose fault it is that he is not a manager for GM.

The only real difference between these two men was their attitudes and willingness to seek and accept responsibility.

Regardless of education or other traits you feel contribute to your problems, personal responsibility is the one attribute that you have complete control over and can employ to add value to yourself. No one can force you to accept it or stop you from seeking it. It is much better to be like Bob than like Carl. They both chose for themselves, just like you can.

Chapter 8

Pride

Pride is internal. It's your feeling of personal worth, the value you place on yourself, and the results of your efforts. You can tell a great deal about a person just by watching how they perform menial tasks, how they dress, and how they conduct themselves, in spite of the rules that are in place. It has nothing to do with cost or fashion. It has to do with self-respect, how they see themselves, and how they wish to be seen by others. Leaders set the standard. If a leader has pride in himself, followers will take pride in their leader and in themselves.

Remember that people will always exceed expectations. If you have pride in yourself, your organization, and in the product or services you produce, it will be reflected by those around you. If your offices or warehouses are clean and orderly, people will work to keep them that way. If you expect to have every piece of work that goes out looking as if it were being presented at a trade show, people will take pride in everything they do everyday. Pride is not a fad. It is an internal part of you and of your organization.

How many times have you heard employees talk with pride about what they do, their supervisors, or the business they work for? How many times have you heard them say, "it's just a job," or "I don't work - I have a job with the Government," or some such demeaning phrase? Pride is what makes people want to contribute. It makes people want to be sure everyone knows where they work, what they do, and who their supervisor is.

There is no such thing as a menial job or one that is not important. If you think there is, just go into a restroom that hasn't been cleaned or work in an office that hasn't had the garbage cans emptied for a week.

A friend of mine relayed this story to me years ago and I have always remembered it. At the time, he was working on the maintenance crew of a large research and development facility. One night he and another worker had to replace a toilet bowl in one of the buildings. After they had installed it, they discovered it wasn't sitting just right. My friend decided it had to be taken out and reset. His companion was incensed to think that a toilet bowl had to be perfect. My friend explained that he had enough pride in himself, his work, and the company for whom they were working, that he wanted to do the best possible job he could to make things right. Needless to say, my friend long ago got off the maintenance crew. He continued to exceed expectations and is successful in many ways. I'm not sure about his helper.

Always take pride in who you are, what you do, and for whom you work. It shows and you will be known for always doing the best you can —nobody will ever ask for more.

Chapter 9

Training

Leaders are trainers, but trainers are not necessarily leaders. If you expect to be a successful supervisor, you have to know how to train other people and be comfortable doing it. If you're not, then you are simply a scheduler. Training is fun if done right. Everyone involved gains from participating in meaningful training, whether instructor or student. One of the essential ingredients to maintaining dignity and self-worth is the feeling that you are always **learning, progressing, and contributing.**

One of the natural laws of leadership is that you are never standing still. You are either progressing or falling behind. Everyday is a challenge just to keep up. **You have to have goals and a training program** for yourself and for your subordinates— not necessarily a formal program in all instances, but a conscious one.

One of the best ways for a leader to gain credibility is to establish a training program for himself and for his staff. You will be hard pressed to find a truly great leader who doesn't read several books a year, can't tell you what is in the morning paper, or can't relate the lessons of the last training session in which he participated. Too many of today's managers think they are fulfilling their responsibilities by simply approving and financing their subordinate's attendance at some seminar or other external training event. Some value can be gained through those mediums, but real long-term, habit-changing value comes from training provided by those with whom you work and the best comes from the person for whom you work. You don't just learn processes and theory. You are learning what the character of your leader is, you are learning what is expected of you, and you are establishing a relationship that serves both of you in the future.

I have spent over three decades being trained and training others. I have been taught by novices and professionals. I have learned that there are two kinds of teachers. First, there are those who are considered professional educators, who are found in colleges and universities or on the training circuit. They educate through hypothetical thinking, debating, analyzing historical events and prognosticating future ones. They are normally removed from the struggles of the day-to-day, one-on-one interpersonal relationships of the workplace.

Second, there are the trainers. They deal in reality and in concrete, identifiable problems. They are seldom referred to as educators, but rather as trainers.

Trainers who really know their trade become leaders. Leaders insure that all of those they train (all of their subordinates) have the knowledge and skills to fulfill their tasks and have the ability to accept the responsibilities that accompany their positions. Leaders personally accept the responsibility of training and the results of their training. They need to know for themselves that everyone has the skills necessary for personal success and to support and strengthen the entire organization.

Training has two simple components. **First, know where you are and where you want to go.** Once you have that information, decide what you need to get you where you want to go. Do you need truck drivers, chemists, managers, or an administrative staff? Each will have a particular set of disciplines to master, both personally and collectively. Initially, the fewer disciplines needed to accomplish the task the better. The second component is a simple, four-step cycle: **plan, resource, conduct, and evaluate.** (See Appendix II–Training Cycle)

Plan what type of training you will need to get where you are going. Make sure you have the time, manpower, materials and equipment (resources). Conduct the training and evaluate the results. If you are not where you want to be as a result of your training, start the cycle over.

As a leader, where do you want to be? Do you have what you need to get there? Does everyone with whom you work have the skills they need? **Being a leader is a never-ending cycle of training and of being trained.** It is not complicated; it is just the realization that neither you nor your subordinates know everything you could or should. It takes a conscious effort to pursue improvement. Never accept the status quo.

To illustrate the value of a leader training a subordinate, I want to relate another personal experience. Over thirty years ago, when I was a young soldier trying to find out where I fit into society, and particularly at that time into my assigned unit, I was approached by my platoon sergeant. The first thing he did was to bolster my dignity and value by making some small comment about how he had observed me and the way I conducted myself. Looking back, I'm not sure exactly what that meant; but at the time, whatever I perceived it to be, I was not going to do anything that would lessen my value in his eyes. He said he wanted me to be his driver, if I thought I could handle the responsibilities.

Well, my vision of having my own three-quarter-ton pickup was overwhelming and the thought of being in charge of the platoon tool trailer, which was pulled by the truck, gave a certain feeling of power. All I could think about at the time was how I had lucked into a soft job. When I eagerly accepted, I was sure all I had to do was wait for him to go to one of his meetings and I could be off for a test drive.

The platoon sergeant told me to meet him in the motor pool after lunch. I assumed it was for a short road test. Upon reaching the assigned place, I found the sergeant with a green binder in his hand. He pulled out a form that was analogous to a check sheet or an owner's manual. We started at the trailer hitch and worked our way forward through the electrical system, the fuel system, the drive train, the braking system, and all of the controls in the cab, to include a 45-minute class on blackout driving conditions. Before that afternoon was over, I had inspected every hose, belt, light, cotter pin and grease joint. I had spent an hour going through maintenance forms and service records. I was introduced to accountability procedures and to my new responsibilities with regard to obtaining the authorized tools, subsequently accounting for, and issuing them from the trailer to platoon members. I fully understood my responsibilities and the consequences of not fulfilling them.

That five-hour training session between my leader and myself probably influenced my future leadership approach and abilities more than any graduate class or general staff college instruction I ever attended. I saw first hand and felt the importance of doing the job right. I was taught to understand the importance of my success to others and the consequences if I failed. That day, I learned what training and leadership meant.

One of the recurring themes you read and hear about leadership, quality, integrity, etc., is that it must start at the top. When was the last time you attended a class presented by your supervisor? More to the point, when did you last give a class to your subordinates? Are you leading or managing?

Training does not need to be drudgery: it can and should be fun. It should be rewarding and challenging. People want and need to be challenged; they feel good when they learn and have a sense of increased value. And remember, if it's done right, the trainer always learns more than the student.

Chapter 10

What Nobody Really Teaches
Hiring and Firing

Two of the hardest things a leader will ever do are to hire and fire employees. You are affecting another person's livelihood, his family, and his entire future. These actions are different from management decisions that affect groups of people. In most instances, when you hire or fire a person, there is a very subjective element to the outcome of your decision. Hiring is important and complicated. It can't adequately be covered here, but my purpose for writing this book would be totally missed if I didn't give what I feel is my best advice on the subject.

Always hire the best-qualified person, someone who is better than yourself, and who is capable of taking over your job. If you hesitate to hire someone better than yourself, you are not a real leader and you are doing yourself and your organization an injustice. Finding the best qualified person is the challenge you have to face based on many factors that will always be

Hiring and Firing

unique to you and to the organization for whom you are working.

When you are faced with having to terminate a person for some reason, ask yourself the following questions: What have I done, or not done, that caused this situation to occur? Did I hire the wrong person? Did I provide enough training, mentoring, and encouragement? Whatever the reason, you (the leader) must take responsibility for someone under your supervision having failed and having to be terminated. Believe me, the experience will greatly improve your hiring and supervision skills.

Whenever an employee won't or can't meet organizational standards, you, the leader, must take disciplinary action that will enforce the standards. Any workforce will always meet or exceed your expectations and standards if properly trained and given the tools required. That is not to say that everyone doesn't need to be refocused, mentored, or helped through some personal or professional problem from time to time. However, those kinds of exchanges can and do take place during routine, informal evaluations and day-to-day interpersonal relations.

Sometimes you will have situations where specific conduct or performance is beyond subtle hints, instruction, or counseling. Do yourself, the offender, and your organization a favor. Don't try and be anyone's friend. They don't need friends at this point: **they need a leader**. When normal, informal actions fail to correct unacceptable and substandard performance, you have to **take positive, unmistakable, quantifiable, and documented action**. That action must establish exactly to what standard and by what date everything needs to be accomplished by the employee in question to be considered acceptable. Don't ever threaten or bully. Stay professional and matter of fact. Review shortcomings, determine necessary actions, and establish time lines necessary for satisfactory performance. If possible, let the person having the problem establish the actions, standards, and timetable he feels are necessary and attainable to bring the problem into compliance.

If the person is unwilling or unable to establish reasonable objectives, then you must establish them yourself. Have the person review and sign a written summation of the requirements and provide him a copy. Insist that nothing less than full compliance is acceptable, or you will weaken your credibility and the organization's ability to be a world-class competitor.

When you determine that there is nothing more you can reasonably do to make that person successful, he no longer is the issue. The primary issue is your remaining **workforce**. They **must see sure, fair, and unmistakable consequences for unacceptable performance or actions**. Take advantage of this unfortunate situation to gain credibility and strengthen your organization.

Chapter 11

Urgency

Urgency is the feeling and belief that something can and must be accomplished expeditiously. Even if you are able to incorporate all of the other traits I've talked about into your leadership style, **without a sense of urgency you can never be a truly successful leader.** I believe that part of the work ethic that has been engineered out of our current workforce is a sense that it does matter if you are first at work, or first to get your assignment done, or the first to complete a project.

The mindset of just putting in your time has evolved. It is going to take a real effort, a reward system overhaul, and a major reeducation of the workforce to regain the thought processes that caused our forefathers to be successful. They would rise and begin work early and stay late just for the accomplishment of their jobs and for the personal rewards that their effort provided. I am not proposing a return to sixteen-hour days, but I believe some policies need serious review–especially policies like everyone (both the good and the bad) getting paid the same and receiving promotions according to the calendar.

Most of what I just mentioned is far beyond the control of new supervisors, so you must simply do what you can to set the example for those with whom you work. **The leader sets the pace for the group.** The difference between a leader and a follower is that the leader knows where he is going, what it should take to get there, and feels as if he should already be there. You cannot be a leader if you are not setting the pace. A sense of urgency is what makes you want to get to work in the mornings, encourage subordinates to excel, provide that edge to your group or team, and distinguish yourself as someone who can be counted on and does not require continuous follow-up.

Never accept that a suspense date or other deadline is the time something must be completed. **A deadline is the last possible time** something is required. Beating deadlines increases your personal value, builds pride in the workforce, and sets real standards.

A friend of mine worked part-time in a local steel mill as a timekeeper while going to college. Unlike most teenagers, and for that matter older workers at that mill, he had a sense of urgency in the things he did. One day he received a call from a plant superintendent who needed some production figures from several divisions for a particular period. My friend didn't realize that process normally took several days to obtain, compile, and submit the information.

Being new, wanting to do a good job, and not knowing any better, he grabbed one of the bikes that was used to get around the plant and started going to the foreman of each division to personally obtain the required information. Within a few hours, he had the information and had compiled it for the

Urgency

superintendent. He then ran a considerable distance across the facility to deliver the requested report.

The superintendent was so impressed with the sense of urgency my friend had displayed that he was given an almost "write-your-own-ticket" job to work around his school schedule along with good pay and tuition assistance.

The moral to this story is that as a result of his sense of urgency and by attacking the requirement rather than just meeting the suspense date, my friend received a good income for many years. He practically received a free education. Over time, that same display of urgency has earned the admiration of many influential leaders. By the way, after graduating from college he joined the military service and became a brigadier general at an early age.

In today's split-second communication age with technologically advanced processes, yesterday's sense of urgency is a minimum requirement for success. Things that just a few years ago took weeks or months to accomplish, today takes days or hours. You can no longer just show up and expect to be retained. You not only have to discover how to keep up yourself, but also how to **bring your staff with you.** If you don't, you will all surely be left behind. You no longer have the option of the "just-hanging-in-there" or "status-quo" way of approaching life and remaining employed, let alone being in demand.

What you need is a sense of urgency with a twenty-first century warp-drive mentality. You also need to instill that same sense of urgency into everyone with whom you work. After all, they also are their own customers and should have a real concern for their own welfare.

Chapter 12

Communication

No review or study of leadership or management would be complete without a discussion about the importance of communication. **Communication, for our purposes, means dialogue and the transfer of information between people** in the workplace. Society is struggling with how to reopen the clogged communication lines that have for so long been primarily one way - from the top to the bottom or from the superior to the subordinate. Both participants in any dialogue need to learn how to communicate in real terms, not just serve as vehicles for sending or receiving information. Communication is not only the transfer of information, but also understanding what it means, how it should be applied, and the expected results of employing the data.

Today's successful leaders are no longer commanders or bosses that can expect their orders and instructions to be followed unquestionably. They are men and women who understand that the controlling, coercive styles of the past no longer work. The communication style of today should be more in the manner of a mentor and negotiator. If you have

Communication

established trust and mutual respect in the workplace, then directives can and should be more informational and educational.

To be truly effective communicators, leaders need to remember the simple definition of leadership: **Getting others to do what you need them to do because they want to.** They will want to do what you need if you are capable of defining needs, proposing courses of action, and marshaling talent and resources. They also realize you are negotiating with them in a fashion that will fulfill their personal and professional needs, your leadership responsibilities, and the organization's goals. Remember, **your main responsibility is to make your superiors and subordinates successful.** By so doing, you are taking care of your real customer—you—in the only real way you can.

Mature adults who know their jobs and have spent years learning their professions don't react well to being addressed as if they were children or of no consequence beyond being part of the machinery. If communication is kept on a professional and mature level, it is received and acted upon at that level. If communication is a two-way street, you gain the benefit of the experience, education, and abilities of those with whom you are communicating.

This is not an attempt to make a communication expert out of anyone, but rather to share a few thoughts on how to communicate in the workplace.

You have two ears and just one mouth; therefore, in any conversation you should listen twice as much as you talk. I have always tried to use the 80-20 rule: Listen at least eighty percent of the time and talk no more than twenty percent.

Most of the time when people ask you for advice, they don't really want it. They just want you to listen, validate, and offer support. When someone seeks your advice or asks you what you think, always ask them what they believe to be the prudent or best course of action. Most of the time they know much more about their jobs and the challenges they face than you do. It only makes sense to listen.

Undoubtedly, you will have a broader view of the situation than most of the people that work for you. Your input is critical, but only to the extent that the employee's ideas conflict with or need to be integrated into other elements of the business. **Even if you have a better idea, keep it to yourself.** If his proposal will get the job done, accept it. The fact that he is implementing his own ideas or process will almost always result in a better end product or service than if he were working on yours or someone else's. What you must do is be astute enough and capable of communicating what you need. At the same time, you must allow and even **facilitate ownership** of each desk, workstation, or process to the maximum extent possible by the person who occupies or performs them.

It is estimated that over 65 percent of performance problems in the workplace result from strained relationships—not from deficits in an individual employee's skill or motivation. These problems are a direct result of inadequate communication between supervisors and employees and between employees themselves. Mediation, while having long been recognized as a vehicle for resolving disputes, has recently burst onto the scene. It is a particularly effective way to address and resolve 80 to 90 percent of workplace conflict before it requires more expensive and divisive procedures such as arbitration or litigation.

Mediation is referred to as magic by many who use it or have been involved in the process. As a long-time certified mediator, I can tell you that it is not magic, but rather a simple process that requires **open and honest communication** between two parties. It involves saying what you mean and meaning what you say. It establishes an atmosphere where, when one person is talking, the other is listening. It requires clarification of meaning and expectations. It is nothing more than being honest and wanting a fair outcome for both parties engaged in the discussion.

As a leader, every communication you have should incorporate those traits mentioned above. It is not only critical that you are an effective communicator, but also that everyone you work with has those skills. The simple, effective tools of the professional mediator in your hands and in the hands of your employees will build better workplace relationships, enhance performance, improve productivity, and add value to you (your real customer) and to everyone else. Simple workplace communication training should be a high priority for you and everyone with whom you work. It will save untold time, money, and unproductive relationships.

The natural tendency of dealing with conflict by either avoiding it or by combating another with whom you are in conflict, is destructive to the people involved and deadly to the organization in which it exists. Open, honest, but sometimes uncomfortable communication is the way leaders resolve problems, build trust, and distinguish themselves from their peers.

For people who recognize the importance of working at relationships, and who want to improve workplace communications, I believe that the study of the book *Managing Differences* by Daniel Dana, PhD, should be mandatory.

PART III

Simple and Successful Leadership

I feel this section is the most important part of the guide. The whole book is intended to be a short read; but far more importantly, you should take a few minutes once or twice a week to review it for the rest of your professional career. The only way you are going to learn, retain, and incorporate new concepts and ways of doing things is through **repetition and review.** You have to do things repeatedly until they become automatic. You have to develop new habits. New habits can only be acquired through repeated review and action.

The absence of review and repetition is why I believe that one- and two-day seminars have minimal impact on significantly changing performance and organizational culture. Many have good ideas and make you feel good while you are attending, but two or three weeks later, most people can't tell you much about them. Beyond remembering the general subject, most individuals are hard pressed to show changes that have taken place as a result of their investment in time and money. That is why throughout this guide, many **simple but important thoughts are printed in bold**. Therefore, if you prefer not to read the whole chapter over and over or don't have the time, you will be able to thumb through and recall the little things that make a difference.

Every new supervisor needs to **know the basics** of **Who, What, When, Where, and Why of leadership** so they can personalize, expand, and perfect their own leadership styles. Also, many experienced managers and leaders tend to let the daily pressures of their jobs overshadow the basic principles of leadership. Or, they forget the little things that mean so much to individuals who work for them. A quick review of these basic truths of interpersonal relationships and leadership will help you to refocus from time to time on the simple things that contribute to a powerful workforce.

Chapter 13

Who: You and the Others

You are your only real customer. You are the only person who has the ability to ensure your personal well being! Everyone else is merely a consumer and a means to an end. They are part of the system that provides you opportunities to make a living, contribute to society, and enjoy the benefits of your efforts. Your future, the future of your family, fellow employees, and your organization depend on how well **you take responsibility—responsibility for your actions and responsibility for the actions of those who work for you.**

Teams and work groups are fine and participative management is a noble sounding concept. But have you ever heard of anyone establishing a Process Action Team to determine the best way to empower everyone and get them involved in shutting down a plant that is going out of business? When was the last time you heard of everyone voting or attending a sensing session to determine who should be let go when the factory orders slow down or contracts are lost? Process Action Teams, empowered workers, quality awards, balloons, and workplace pep rallies are not realistic when the survival of careers and businesses are at stake. If you truly believe you are working with mature professionals, then you should treat them like adults, not like high school students you're trying to con so you can get a little more production out of them.

Here are two examples for you to think about. The first involves what used to be the McDonnell-Douglas helicopter plant in Mesa, Arizona. A few years ago, I visited that plant. There were signs everywhere celebrating everything. It seemed like there were employees of the month, week, day, and hour. The main entrance was decorated with handmade signs and balloons. It looked like a high school homecoming. McDonnell-Douglas was up to its proverbial ears in the total-quality, feel-good, celebrate-everything craze of the 90s. Today there is no McDonnell-Douglas helicopter plant. They spent too much time celebrating yesterday's successes and not enough time looking for tomorrow's opportunities and challenges. They obviously had other management problems, but the efforts and resources directed at empowering employees were wasted.

The second example involves the military and, I suspect, other government agencies. They have spent millions of dollars on total-quality, get-everybody-involved programs and competitions, but to what end? Jobs have been lost or contracted out. Bases have closed and all but one service can't enlist the numbers of recruits they need. The one service that keeps achieving its goals is the Marine Corps. Why? They treat their members like adults, they maintain high standards, and they do not compromise or make excuses.

Be a leader, not a historian. It doesn't matter what you did yesterday. The only thing that matters is what you are doing today and what you are planning for tomorrow and beyond. Real leaders are visionaries. They learn from the past but concentrate on the future.

The reality is that if you are a better leader than anyone else in the office, plant, or industry, and you and your group produce more and better products or services, then you are adding value to the organization and its stakeholders. By doing so you are also protecting your future and the future of your fellow workers. No one will be able to save your job if your value is less than others who offer the same or better efforts and results for less cost. Forget about celebrating yesterday's successes. Spend your energy on tomorrow's. Don't worry who gets the credit. Success and security are what leaders pursue, not parties and personal recognition.

Empower yourself. Be the Chief Executive Officer of "Yourself, Inc.," the most important enterprise in the world. Don't wait to be told what to do; and don't spend a lot of time and energy on eye wash. **Just look for what needs to be done and do it.** General Norman Schwarzkopf put it this way: "When in charge, take charge!"

Always remember, a leader can never be more successful than the least successful of his subordinates. Your success must be measured by the totality of your area of responsibility. **Leadership is not a high office, but an office of high responsibility.**

You will hear this said several different ways, but the one easiest to remember is, "never take yourself too seriously." Remember that no one is irreplaceable, and someday **you will be replaced**. The only questions are when it will happen, who will replace you, and where you will be going. Remember who your customer really is and **do the best you can** for yourself. By so doing, **everyone around you will benefit.** Never think that you are so intelligent, so important, or so badly needed that you can push your way into a position of unquestioned authority. Also, **have some fun.** People who enjoy their work are always more successful than those who just work at their jobs.

In a position of leadership, you must accept the fact that when you assume authority over other peoples' lives, they in turn have a right to scrutinize yours. You cannot be one type of person on one occasion and another type on another. **Being a real leader is a way of life,** not just a title or an eight-to-five responsibility.

Being a good leader also requires another dimension of character; it requires you to **be a good follower.** You cannot be a good leader until you have mastered the discipline of being a follower. What does being a good follower mean? It means that you should never expect to attain more respect or loyalty from subordinates than you have and demonstrate for your superiors. An old saying goes something like this: **As long as you work for a person and accept pay from him, you must be loyal to that person**. Nothing is as valuable to a leader than the loyalty of the staff he has working for him. If you are not loyal to your superiors, how can you expect loyalty from your subordinates?

The Others

Who are the others? First, they are the people who hire and pay you. I have already talked about what you owe them and how you should treat them. Remember, your employer may like you and even be your friend, but he has superiors or stakeholders whose needs and desires will always trump the personal relationship you have with him when the chips are down. That isn't a bad thing; it is just a fact that you need to understand. The only thing you can do is **ensure** that your employer and the stakeholders, whoever **they** are, **understand what your value represents to them.**

Secondly, others are **the people whom you lead**. These are the men and women who give you all they have and expect you to look out for their welfare. You have the responsibility to hire the best possible workforce you can. Always hire the best-qualified people. Give them all the resources possible, train them, give them trust and support, make sure they understand your expectations, and then get out of their way.

Two of the twentieth century's most successful and notable leaders, one from the military and the other from the civilian sector, basically said the same thing in this regard, but in slightly different ways. I believe they are worth repeating; no better advice can be given.

> "Never tell people how to do things. Tell them what to do and they will surprise you with their ingenuity."
>
> —General George S. Patton

> "The way to harness the power of these people is not to protect them, not to sit on them, but to turn them loose, let them go, and get the management layers off their backs, the bureaucratic shackles off their feet, and the functional barriers out of their way."
>
> —Jack Welch, CEO, General Electric

Numerous studies have proved time and again that **people will react positively to kindness, respect, trust, and high expectations.** The reverse is also true: **They will act negatively to degrading comments, demeaning treatment, a lack of trust, and low or no expectations.** Treat people like adults, give them freedom to contribute, recognize them appropriately, and you will find a force most new supervisors and managers take years to discover, if ever. Remember the newest, least-paid employees hold your success in their hands. Maybe not today or next week, but sometime. **Every day you make allies or enemies** (no one is neutral) and everyone has opportunities to help or hinder any operation. **Allies make a much better workforce.**

Chapter 14

What

Leadership qualities make the difference between people who are winners and those who go through life wondering why others are getting all of the breaks. They make the difference between those who know where they are going and have a plan to get there and those who simply wait, follow, or hope. **Leaders are risk takers; they have self-awareness and courage to step up and step out.** They don't look for or make excuses. Leaders understand that mistakes and failures lead to success.

> "It is far better to dare mighty things, to win glorious triumphs, even though checkered by failure, than to take rank with those poor spirits who neither enjoy much nor suffer much, because they live in the gray twilight that knows not victory nor defeat."
>
> —Theodore Roosevelt

Education was recognized long ago as vital to success. No longer will just hard work get you the positions you deserve. It is not for me to make a case that leaders have to be well educated and that education is a never-ending journey. However, Americans have a fascination with education; they often mistakenly confuse education with intelligence and wisdom. **Beware of putting too much importance in the initials behind someone's name.** A real education can only partly be obtained in classrooms and on campuses. Treat everyone as if he has a PhD, and you'll find an army of people with doctorates in quality, service, loyalty, common sense, and dedication.

Training is something that will happen no matter what type of position you have. But **leadership takes a personal commitment to excellence**, conscious effort, mature ability, and a confidence to put yourself up for ridicule. An ongoing training program is necessary for any leader and critical to his subordinates. Make sure you **have a professional development program for you and your staff**. Everybody needs and appreciates opportunities to learn and progress.

Leadership is always treating other people with respect and dignity. It is selflessness in pursuit of goals beyond personal recognition and gain. Leaders, real leaders, **have integrity, unquestioned honesty, and are always ethical. Leaders always take pride in themselves, in their associates, and in their organizations.** They are always mindful of the needs of those for whom they are responsible. They **ensure that subordinates are trained** and have the resources to be successful. They also ensure that they themselves have the technical competencies required for their positions.

Leaders understand the importance of every human being and the qualities that make up an organization. They also have the courage to take sometimes painful and unpopular actions and make decisions that have to be made for the good of the organization and its collective membership. They believe that while everyone is valuable, no one is irreplaceable.

Finally, leaders communicate. They communicate formally through inspections, performance reviews, training, correspondence, and meetings. They communicate informally through acknowledgments, greetings, mentoring, and social events. They communicate with everyone every chance they get.

Leaders have goals—goals for themselves and for their organizations. They communicate their goals, they display them, and report on the status of them. They embrace change. They always believe that tomorrow has to be, and will be, better than yesterday.

Leadership is something that no one can force you to take and something that no one but you can destroy.

Simple tips

- **Have your expectations published and posted where everyone can see them. (See Appendix V—Feedback Sample)**

It doesn't matter what you call them—goals, mission statement, vision, tactical plan, or any of a dozen other names. For the new supervisor, what you need to know is where you are, where you are going, what it takes to get there, and what is expected of everybody involved in the journey.

- **Have a simple management control system for you and everyone that works for you.**

Internal controls need not be fancy or particularly sophisticated. A simple checklist will usually suffice, a list that you can spot check to make sure the right things are being done, and to your standard. The first thing any auditor or inspector will look for is your internal controls. If you have them, you are always ahead of the game. But more importantly, it is an excellent and sure way to keep up with your responsibilities.

- **Have an open door policy**

Always be accessible. Don't let people use this policy to gossip or look for sympathy, but make sure everyone knows that if they have a real problem that just can't get resolved through normal actions, you are available. Some form of suggestion program will always pay dividends. (See Appendix VI—Feedback Sample.)

- **Don't give anyone the solution to a problem; help find it.**

One of the most important things a leader can do is help others find the answers to their problems. That's what mentoring is all about. New supervisors, particularly, just tell people how to do things, but then what have they learned? It's analogous to the parable of giving a hungry man a fish to eat versus teaching him to fish. Real leaders are known for the quality of the people they have working for them and for the strength and skills that they have. Leaders teach people how to research, interpret, and implement independently. Leaders surround themselves with people who are capable of replacing them. **You only build a winning organization by building a self-reliant staff.**

- **Never have a meeting over one hour.**

Attention and interest spans for most people are measured in minutes. Anything you discuss after the first twenty or thirty minutes has minimal impact. **What value are you adding when you are doing business with yourself?** Always have an agenda published ahead of time and let people know you will stick to it. Soon, important things will appear on the agenda and the other things will disappear. **Stay focused on results** not on processes. Minutes should always be kept on official meetings and assignments should always be reported on. **Insist on accountability** for completion of any assignment given.

- **Always, always keep your word**

Trust is hard to gain and easy to lose. **Never say anything you don't mean. Never promise anything you can't personally produce.** Mistakes will by made by you and others. Always immediately acknowledge them, review what caused them, and take steps to prevent future occurrences. Take advantage of these learning opportunities. Concentrate on problems, not on personalities.

- **Always remember you can never be successful unless everybody else is.**

This thought is spread throughout this guide on purpose and reiterated over and over because in today's society, it is too common for everyone to think they are doing just fine, but others are slacking. The point has to be made to leaders, supervisors, managers, and employees that **everyone has to be successful to survive.**

- **You set the standards, pace, and expectations of the organization.**

Everyone is influenced by the actions of the leader. If you set high standards and enforce them, people will work hard to meet and exceed them. No one wants to be left behind or be the cause of failure. Everyone wants to be part of an energized, progressive, and successful organization. **Everyone wants and needs to have a real leader to follow.** A real leader, not a cheerleader.

Chapter 15
When

Now is the time for you to accept the fact that times have changed. Nobody else can look out for you, and the sooner you start adding value to your name, service, and leadership abilities, the more secure your future will be.

Leaders are always leaders. If you pretend to be a leader, you will be found out sooner or later. If you just got assigned or promoted into a leadership position because you are a good worker but don't want to be a leader or take responsibility for others, do yourself and everyone else a favor and don't try and fake it. **Not everyone can or should be a leader.** Many of the greatest people in history were not leaders; most people aren't. In every organization, there are many people who are extremely valuable and contribute, but they are not leaders. They are hard working, dedicated, honest, and want to be part of a well-led organization. These people deserve the best leadership you can provide. They will be loyal and contribute in many ways if they are simply afforded dignity and shown appreciation.

Leadership positions are not given for personal gratification, but to enable people to serve those whom they lead.

Daily

• **Acknowledge everyone who works for you.** Make sure to greet everyone in the workplace. A simple, "good morning, how are things going?" will improve the environment a great deal. It gives people a chance to let you know if something really is important to them. It lets them know that you know they are at work and that you appreciate their contributions.

• **If a reprimand is required,** never let the day end without taking appropriate action. It won't be any easier tomorrow. If you and/or others are aware that some infraction has occurred which calls for some type of reprimand, **sure, swift, and fair action is your only course.** Good leaders are known for their decisiveness, not for threatening and then taking indecisive actions. Face the hard tasks first!

Weekly

• At least twice a week, you need to **have a short (stand-up) meeting** with your first-line subordinates and insist that they all do the same with theirs. They need to hear from you personally how you think things are going. You need to talk to them and **emphasize the things that are important** to you. Give everyone a chance to ask questions and get any clarification they need. More importantly, it gives you and them a chance to coordinate as a group and to make sure everyone is in step working toward the same goals.

Team leaders, if not kept focused, tend to personalize goals that sometimes are not as supportive to your organizational goals as they could be. Nobody can go far astray in two or three days. An open, honest, and continual flow of information is critical. **Rumors cease if the facts are out** for everyone to see. **It's impossible to give employees too much information about things that affect their lives.**

- **Praise.** Never let a week go by that you don't say or do something positive and encouraging to each of your subordinates. It could be a word, a short note, or a phone call that is neither formal nor made for any particular reason other than to reinforce the person's value to you and the organization. Conversely, never let a week go by when someone who is not meeting your expectations is left unaware of it. Let the person know so he can take appropriate corrective action.

Monthly

- Key to leadership is inspecting. Leaders who are really on top of their responsibilities personally inspect their subordinates' work. A good rule of thumb is to look at, review, sample, or spot check five to ten percent of their work. If you don't have that kind of time, then at least inspect something. There are many reasons why you should do this. If you routinely take a random sample of your employees' work, they will always have everything the best they can. It stops wasting time just getting ready for inspections or audits. You should be ready for an audit all the time!

Additionally, your people will feel that if the boss inspects their work, it must be important. They will complete tasks to a much higher standard than if the auditors come in every year or so. **Things that get inspected get done.**

You will always learn other things while inspecting that you would never have guessed or thought to ask. Inspecting also requires you to learn what your employees are doing and gains their respect by not expecting them to accomplish tasks you aren't at least familiar with.

Monthly, informal performance appraisals keep you and your subordinates on the same track towards success. Adjustments (improvements) in work habits are easily made in small, non-threatening increments. Additionally, formal appraisals are easy to complete and normally successful due to the absence of any surprises.

Quarterly

• The best way to obtain unit or organizational cohesion is to ensure that everybody knows what the organizational goals are and how each person, section, or division contributes to their attainment. No better use of time can be spent than to have a quarterly organizational meeting attended by every employee. It takes one or two hours to review the past quarter, the results of the work that has been accomplished, the progress towards future goals, and to forecast upcoming events and challenges.

A quarterly meeting is a great time to let people ask questions and hear directly from the "boss" without the information filters that are inevitable in any organization. It gives you a chance to highlight things that are particularly important to you and keeps everybody talking the same language. For one time, every three months, everyone in your organization is on the same foot and is thinking the same way. It also lets everybody see who they work with and gain an appreciation for what they are a part of.

A quarterly meeting is also important to make sure that everyone understands what everybody else does and how each contributes. It puts a face or name to the illusive "they" that causes so many problems in most organizations. Once people find out and understand that every section or division has the same kind of challenges and frustrations that they do, they start looking for ways to be more helpful and therefore more valuable.

It's not unusual, even in small organizations, that some people don't fully understand the way what they do affects others and contributes to the business, end product, or service. All they may know is what flows over their desk or where to stack the boxes. It may seem like a big investment in man-hours, but consider how much time is taken by the average employee in a three-month period chasing rumors or just wondering what's going on. You will develop real synergy with little effort by keeping everyone informed.

- Depending on where you work and the type of business you are in, quarterly may be too long a time between **formal status reports**. At least **every three months** every supervisor and manager should have to stand and account for their actions. Practically everything worth doing can and should be quantified and charted. Everyone has to know exactly where they are in relation to your expectations and the organization's goals. Are they ahead or behind of schedule, above or below the goals, and why? How many widgets did they process the last quarter? How does that relate to current, previous quarters, and last year's forecasts? If you don't **know exactly where you are,** how can you tell if you're going to get where you are going on time? If everyone knows and can see on a chart how their efforts are contributing in relation to organizational goals, they have a real sense of accomplishment. You also know how everyone is doing.

Another basic truth of leadership is captured in the following:

> "When we deal in generalities, we shall never succeed.
> When we deal in specifics, we shall rarely have a failure.
> When performance is measured, performance improves.
> When performance is measured and reported, the rate of performance accelerates."
> —Thomas S. Monson

- Professional Development. At least once a quarter some form of training should be conducted or sponsored by the leadership of the organization. Training does not necessarily have to be job related. Educational experiences afford employees a realization that their value is being increased by you, the leader.

Semiannually

- At least twice a year, everyone should receive some formal reward or recognition. A raise, a letter of appreciation, perhaps a gift certificate—something they can take home and share with their family and friends. For such a small price, the benefits in loyalty far outweigh the effort and cash value.

- Reevaluate roles and responsibilities. Conduct progress evaluations and present opportunities to have, one-on-one, confidential communication.

Annually

- At least once a year, you should evaluate your own situation. Evaluate your educational status, your career progression, your contributions to the business for which you work, and your role as a leader. Review and update near and long-term goals. Make sure you have a plan that will always ensure accomplishment of your goals and ensure your own well being. Remember who the customer is. If you spend as much time worrying about yourself and about your future as you are supposed to worry about everybody else, both they and you will be successful. Evaluate courses of action you need to consider and make any adjustments or changes necessary.

- Closely review each of your subordinates. Are they making appropriate progress in their fields? Do they have the education and credentials for their positions? What actions can you take to assist them in accomplishing the things they need to have a successful career? Annual performance ratings should be nothing more than recapping and dating your previous monthly reviews.

Chapter 16

Where

A critical principle of leadership that is often overlooked or ignored is what the military calls "seeing the battlefield." In the civilian and corporate world, it is called **management by walking around (MBWA)**. You have to **get out and see what is really going on. Talk to people.** The higher in any organization you go, the more important it is to **make sure you know firsthand** what the line employees are doing and thinking. Operations two or three levels down are seldom, if ever, what you think they are. Attitudes come to you through filters, and you find yourself living in a false world and then wondering why things aren't going like you think they should. It is almost guaranteed that every time you spend a hour or so visiting the floor, production line, or warehouse, you will learn something that will help you be a better leader and improve your organization.

The leader has to be seen by the employees. A few minutes spent dropping by the break room and visiting over a cup of coffee will do more for morale and for building trust than all of the team-building courses you can buy.

- The subject of "Where" also has to address from where you lead.

You **lead from the front and in person**, not from your office, computer, or through the mail.

You lead in public. However, never chastise, correct, or reprimand anyone in public. **Praise in public—reprimand in private.**

- You are a leader all of the time. Never forget that leadership is a way of life. It is a part of your character and the way you look to others. Always remember, **you aren't what you think you are, but rather what you think—you are.**

Chapter 17

Why

You have only two choices today—lead or follow. You have to choose. Either is noble and both are necessary. If you choose to follow, then make sure you are the best follower in the world. Most people are actually happier without the added responsibilities of personnel problems, payroll, procurement, sales, manufacturing, shipping, accounting, and a thousand other details that leaders deal with every day.

I have had, by most standards, a successful professional life. I started out working in a potato warehouse running a crew that loaded hundred-pound sacks of potatoes into train cars. Over the years I progressed from position to position and from sector to sector. As I come to the end of my current career and prepare to launch into my next, I have responsibility for several hundreds of millions of dollars worth of equipment and an annual budget of tens of millions of dollars. I only mention this because without following, as best I could, the simple, basic truths that are outlined in this guide, I would probably still be loading train cars. The same could also be true without the professional, dedicated, and loyal cadre of supporters that I have been fortunate enough to be associated with throughout my life.

Never, ever underestimate the value of other people to your personal success. If you are a leader—lead; if you are a follower—follow; but whichever is best for you, **do it with a vengeance for success** for everyone. Followers, by supporting their leaders and the organization that pays them, add real value to everyone, but particularly to themselves. The best leader in the world is of little value if there isn't anybody to lead.

It doesn't matter if you are the CEO of an international corporation or the leader of a two-person team. **If you are the leader, you are responsible** for the attainment of the organization's goals and the success and well being of the members over which you have responsibility. The future of the entire enterprise, regardless of its size, is in your hands.

Excuses are for managers, not for leaders!

When it is all said and done, you have only yourself to blame or credit for your lot in life. If along the way you have helped others take pride in their work, become successful, and provide a service to society, then you have accomplished more than most. You can proudly say, "I did the best I could and I am responsible for the outcome."

The few basic truths of leadership I have outlined here will never change. They will always serve you well, no matter what your position or goals. You will always be able to look anyone in the eye, no matter where you meet them, and be proud of what you have done without excuses or regrets.

Conclusion

We are where we are! It serves no useful purpose now to spend time making excuses or attempting to affix blame for the state we are in. It is only useful to evaluate our current situation and determine the best way to repair and regain the dignity and leadership that is essential for ourselves and the others in our society. By incorporating the truths as outlined in this guide, leaders and organizations can secure their futures in a way that is impossible through other means. Additionally, it will significantly aid in restoring those admirable, personal traits that originally led America to greatness.

Leaders, by example, must illustrate the fact that we are all dependent on each other's success and well being. We can no longer afford to subscribe to the illusion that we are part of a flock of unfortunates who will be cared for by some elite shepherd. Each of us has unique talents and contributions to make. We need to stop waiting for permission to take control of ourselves. Step up, and accept personal responsibility. We need to prove our individual value to everyone with whom we come in contact by demonstrating our abilities and genuine concern for their welfare. By so doing, we greatly improve our abilities to secure our future and those of our associates.

I would like to impart one last thought: The truths outlined herein need not be employed exclusively in the workplace. They have universal applicability to interpersonal relationships. They are as valid at home and in the community as anywhere else.

> "An Army of Deer led by a lion is much more to be feared than an Army of lions led by a Deer."
>
> —Macedonian Proverb

Appendix I

Trust Cycle

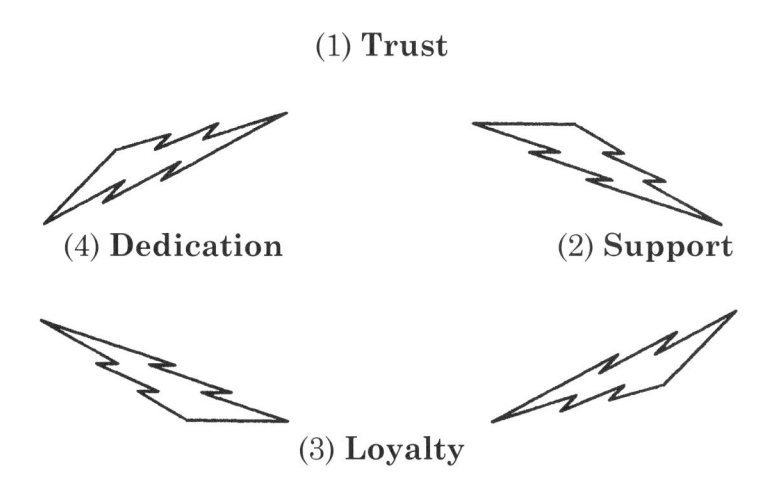

(1) **Trust**

(4) **Dedication** (2) **Support**

(3) **Loyalty**

It is up to you, the leader, to earn the trust of your subordinates. You must trust them to do what you expect and believe them capable of doing. You start by trusting them with small, relatively risk-fee actions. As they demonstrate their capabilities and trustworthiness, you increase their freedom and responsibilities until you both have established a real trust in each other—the leader in the abilities and character of the follower, and the follower in the sincerity and integrity of the leader.

Building trust leads to mutual respect and support that goes beyond typical superior-subordinate relationships. Support then leads to a sense of loyalty that both parties feel towards each other and towards the trust that they have established.

When real loyalty and a sense of responsibility are established between two people, each party will go to great lengths to support and maintain the relationship. It is almost an automatic human response.

Once support and loyalty to a person and organization have been demonstrated over and over, there ensues a profound dedication to continue those positive and mutually rewarding alliances. Continual, dedicated performance results in ever-increasing trust, support, and loyalty.

This simple cycle illustrates why you will always find openness, honesty, trust, and mutual respect in the best organizations. Without these attributes as part of your personal and organizational culture, you only go through the motions of leadership and your employees are going through the motions of support, loyalty, and dedication. No amount of motivational training or new program implementation will compensate for their absence. Moreover, if they are not present, even if only subconsciously, everyone knows it and reacts accordingly.

Appendix II

Training Cycle

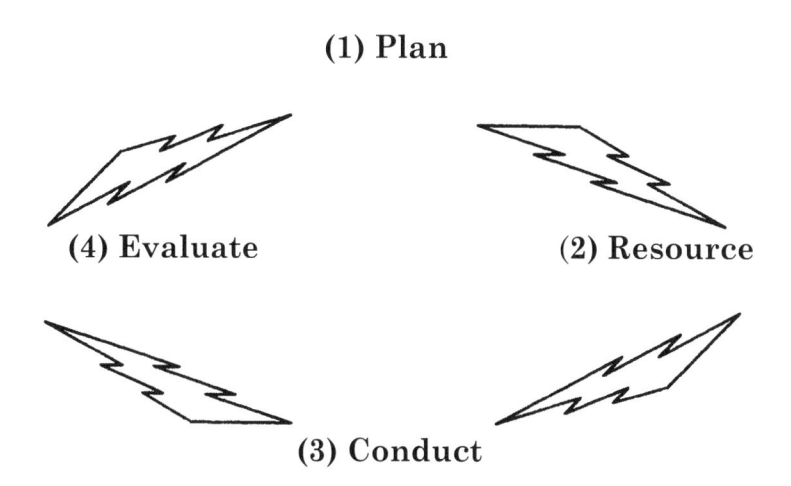

(1) Plan

(4) Evaluate (2) Resource

(3) Conduct

    Plan what type of training you will need to take you where you are going. Make sure you have the time, manpower, materials, and equipment (resources). Conduct the training and evaluate the results. If you are not where you want to be as a result of your training, start the cycle over.

    As a leader, where do I want to be? Do I have what I need to get there? Does everyone I work with have the skills they need? **Being a leader is a never-ending cycle of training and of being trained.** It is not complicated; it is just the realization that neither you nor your subordinates know everything you could or should. It takes a conscious effort to pursue improvement. **Never accept the status quo.**

Appendix III

Leader's Checklist

Daily
- Acknowledge everyone who works for you.
- Reprimand or take corrective action if necessary.
- Face the hard tasks.

Weekly
- Two or three short coordination meetings (stand up) with every subordinate. Emphasize expectations.
- Positive reinforcement (encouragement/praise) for every subordinate.

Monthly
- Inspect
- Informal Performance Appraisal

Quarterly
- Organizational Meeting
- Formal Status Report
- Professional Development Training (formal or informal)

Semiannually
- Formally award or recognize subordinates.
- Reevaluate roles and responsibilities.

Annually
- Evaluate your own situation.
- Review each subordinate's value and progress.

Appendix IV

Recommended Reading

Daniel Dana, PhD, *Managing Differences: How to Build Better Relationships at Work and Home,* MTI Publications, 10210 Robinson Street, Overland Park, Kansas 66212-2512 (www.mediationworks.com)

Bob Nelson, *1001 Ways To Reward Employees– Money Isn't Everything, Low-Cost Ideas, Proven Strategies, Achievement Awards, Contests, Time Off, Case Studies, Praise.* Workman Publishing, New York.

William C. Byham, PhD, with Jeff Cox, *Zapp! The Lightning of Empowerment–How to Improve Quality, Productivity, and Employee Satisfaction,* Fawcett Columbine, New York.

Wess Roberts, PhD, *Leadership Traits of Attila the Hun,* Doubleday, New York.

Appendix V

Expectations Sample

Principles of the Widget Division

We, the members of the Widget Division, subscribe to the following principles:

1. Commit at all levels to continually strive to improve our products and services through elimination of process delays, errors, and duplication.
2. Foster pride in ownership, and take individual responsibility for our actions.
3. Know and value those consumers for which we provide products and services and make every effort to exceed their expectations.
4. Involve everyone in problem identification and resolution.
5. Promote environmental and safety improvement both inside and outside of the workplace.
6. Support professional development and training programs that provide the skills and knowledge necessary to build confidence and ensure everyone's success.
7. Use statistical processes to measure and improve our effectiveness, contributions to each other, and our organization.
8. Eliminate fear and apprehension in order to promote open, honest communication and break down organizational barriers.

9. Treat every person we meet, work with, or provide our services or products to with respect and dignity.
10. Always pursue excellence in our work, personal, and professional associations.
11. Refuse to participate in or be associated with any activities that are not supportive of our division and every one of its members.

"Everyone's Success Is Our Own"

Appendix VI
Feedback Sample
Widget Division

Consumer Service Comment

The goals and expectations of the leadership of the Widget Division are to maintain unequaled value to the consumers of our products and to our employees who produce them. By doing so, we all serve you and ourselves in securing a better future. If we have not done that, we would appreciate knowing what you believe would improve our value and your continued reliance on us.

Was the product or service of high quality?

☐ Yes ☐ No

Was it provided—
Courteously? ☐ Yes ☐ No
Promptly? ☐ Yes ☐ No

Add your comments: _____
_____
_____
_____

If you could make changes to increase our value to you, what would you do? _____
_____
_____
_____

Would you like to be contacted? ☐ Yes ☐ No

Name: _____

Date: _____ Telephone(optional)_____

Address:_____

Note: Employees or consumers of services or products from any organization should have a vehicle that will give them access to the leadership. Leaders must solicit and respond to the needs and concerns of those they serve and to whom they provide services or products.

Selected Bibliography

Michael Beer, Bert Spector, Paul R. Lawrence, D. Quinn Mill, Richard E. Walton, *Human Resource Management,* A General Manager's Perspective, The Free Press A Division of Macmillan, Inc., New York, 1985

Daniel Dana, PhD, *Managing Differences,* How to Build Better Relationships at Work and Home, MTI Publication, Overland Park, Kansas 66212-2512, 1997

Peter F. Drucker, *The Practice of Management,* Harper & Row, Publishers, New York, Grand Rapids, Philadelphia, St. Louis, San Francisco, London, Singapore, Sydney, Tokyo, Toronto, 1954, 1982

Janet Lowe, *Jack Welch Speaks,* Wisdom from the World's Greatest Business Leader, John Wiley & Sons, Inc. New York

Deborah Shapley, *Promise and Power,* The Life and Times of Robert McNamara, Little, Brown & Company (Canada) Limited, 1993

Mary Walton, *The Deming Management Method,* Perigee Books, New York, 1986

About the Author

Bart O. Davis is the owner of B&K Solutions, specialists in alternative dispute resolution, workplace organization, and conflict resolution. A certified mediator and negotiator, he started doing volunteer work as a mediator in his spare time. That work developed into a vocation. With extensive training and experience in leadership, he spent significant time and resources over twenty years attempting to implement so-called "modern management systems." Mr. Davis believes that the qualities of leadership and dignity can give people the capacity to identify and rectify the majority of daily struggles and worker distraction in both the civilian and government sectors. In this book Mr. Davis shares truths of leadership that increase the value of the people who embrace them while helping others achieve progress as well.

Mr. Davis served in the military during the Vietnam War. He obtained a direct commission and retired as a Colonel from the US Army after 34 years of military service. He welcomes comments and inquiries on the topics of dispute resolution, organizational management—and leadership that really works.

Inquiry

Send your questions or comments to—

    Bart O. Davis
    B&K Solutions, L.C.
    7049 Greenborough Dr.
    PO Box 664
    Midvale, Utah 84047

    1 800 688-LEAD (5323)
    801 566-4596
    Fax 801 233-0336
    Address on Internet: www.leaderswin.com

From—
    Name: _____

    Position: _____

    Organization: _____
    _____

    Department/Division: _____
    _____

    Address: _____

    City/State/Zip:_____

    Telephone:_____

    Email: _____

        —or attach your business card.

Number of copies	Price per copy	Amount
_____	$14.95	$ _____
	Add $1.50 per copy for shipping & handling	$ _____
	Total enclosed	$ _____

Ship to:

Name: _____

Position: _____

Organization: _____
_____

Department/Division: _____
_____

Address: _____

City/State/Zip: _____

Telephone: _____

Email: _____

Send this form (or a copy) with payment to—

  B&K Solutions, L.C.
  7049 Greenborough Dr.
  PO Box 664
  Midvale, UT 84047

—or fax your order with your company purchase order to 801 233-0336.

Special pricing available for 10 or more copies to the same address. Call 801 566-4596.